Date: 1/22/15

J 510 MAR
Marsico, Katie,
Kitchen math /

KITCHEN MATH

KATIE MARSICO

Lerner Publications Company • Minneapolis

Lerner Publications Company
A division of Lerner Publishing Group, Inc.
241 First Avenue North
Minneapolis, MN 55401 USA

For reading levels and more information, look up this title at www.lernerbooks.com.

Photo Acknowledgments
The images in this book are used with the permission of: © iStockphoto.com/RuthBlack, p. 1; © Cathy Yeulet/Hemera/ Thinkstock, p. 4; © iStockphoto.com/spxChrome, 5,9, 15, 17, 21, 25, (notebook); © Jrtmedia/Dreamstime.com, p. 5 (chocolate sauce); © Karam Miri/Dreamstime.com, p. 5 (measuring cup); © Maike Jessen/Picture Press/Getty Images, p. 6; © iStockphoto.com/alubalish, 7, 9, 13, 15, 23, 25 (torn paper); © iStockphoto.com/MrLonelyWalker, p. 7 (spoons); © margouillat photo/Shutterstock.com, p. 7 (spaghetti); © iStockphoto.com/iamsania, p. 7 (sauce); © Matilda Lindeblad/ Johner Images/Getty Images, p. 8; © iStockphoto.com/campbellstock, p. 9 (soda bottle); © Andersen Ross/Alamy, p. 10; © Paper Street Design/Shutterstock.com, p. 11 (pan); © iStockphoto.com/Valuykin, p. 11 (bananas); © JupiterImages/ Stockbyte/Getty Images, p. 12; © Image Source/Getty Images, p. 13 (bars); © iStockphoto.com/GMVozvd, p. 14; © Tetra Images - Vstock LLC/Brand X Pictures/Getty Images, p. 15 (turkey and oven); © Andersen Ross/Blend Images/Getty Images, p. 16; © iStockphoto.com/nkbimages, p. 17 (timer); © iStockphoto.com/Sarah Doow, p. 17 (cookies); © Jay Blakesberg/ UpperCut Images/Getty Images, p. 18; © iStockphoto.com/janeff, p. 19; © robert Deuschman/Taxi/Getty Images, p. 20; © iStockphoto.com/kontrast-fotodesign, p. 21 (smoothie); © Fuse/Getty Images, p. 22; © Lisa F. Young/iStock/Thinkstock, p. 23 (fudge); © iStockphoto.com/kupicoo, p. 24; © etiennevoss/iStock/Thinkstock, p. 25 (carrots); © iStockphoto.com/Jason_V, p. 26; © iStockphoto.com/Nemida, p. 27 (lemons); © Stacey Newman/iStock/Thinkstock, p. 28; © iStockphoto.com/RuthBlack, p. 29.

Front Cover: © Bruce Laurance/Blend Images/Getty Images

Back Cover: © iStockphoto.com/jocic

Main body text set in Conduit ITC Std 14/18. Typeface provided by International Typeface Corp.

Library of Congress Cataloging-in-Publication Data

Marsico, Katie, 1980–
        Kitchen math / by Katie Marsico.
            page   cm — (Math everywhere!)
        Includes index.
        ISBN 978-1-4677-1883-7 (lib. bdg. : alk. paper)
        ISBN 978-1-4677-4695-3 (eBook)
        1. Mathematics—Juvenile literature. 2. Cooking—Juvenile literature. I. Title.
    QA40.5.M3773 2015
    510—dc23   2013037671

Manufactured in the United States of America
1 – CG – 7/15/14

TABLE OF CONTENTS

FROM CUPS TO CUPCAKES

Math is exciting! It shapes our world. Want proof? Simply step into your kitchen. Then just try making a tasty treat or meal without using math. That's hard to do!

Maria knows that she needs math to cook. She also knows how to make incredible chocolate cupcakes. Maria follows her grandma's secret recipe, of course!

What's Grandma's special touch?
Promise not to tell? Okay, okay.
Maria's grandma adds 16 fluid ounces
(473 milliliters) of chocolate syrup to
her cupcake batter.

Grandma has another secret too. She tells
Maria that she always uses exact measurements.
Otherwise, she would end up with a big gooey mess
instead of a delicious dessert!

Maria is almost ready to get cooking. Chocolate syrup? Check! Measuring cup?
Check! It's time to bake like a pro—and to do a little conversion along the way.

Uh-oh! Maria's measuring cup doesn't show fluid ounces!
But Maria knows that

1 cup (237ml) = 8 fluid ounces (237 ml).

**So how many cups of
chocolate syrup should
go into her mouthwatering
cupcakes?**

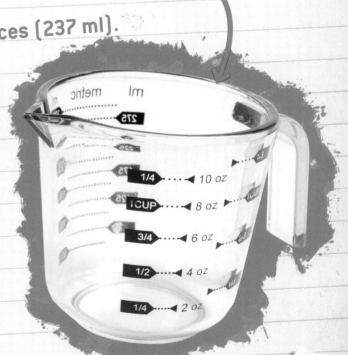

Check your answers to all questions on pages 30–31.

SPOONFULS OF SAUCE

Friday is pasta night at Carlo's house. Sometimes his family eats spaghetti. Other times, they munch on macaroni. Either way, it's the sauce that makes the meal come together. Their yummy sauce recipe has been in Carlo's family for more than 100 years!

Tonight Carlo is helping his dad cook the sauce. Carlo heads to the pantry to gather a couple of ingredients. The first is ¼ cup (59 ml) of tomato paste. The second is 1½ tablespoons (22 ml) of olive oil.

Next, Carlo hunts for measuring utensils. There's just one problem. The measuring cups are in the dishwasher. So is the tablespoon. Must Carlo's family postpone their pasta dinner?

No way! Dad simply grabs the teaspoon.

He says 48 teaspoons (237 ml) = 1 cup.
And 3 teaspoons (15 ml) = 1 tablespoon.

How many teaspoons of tomato paste does Carlo need? How many teaspoons of olive oil?

DO THE MATH!

Imagine you are making meatballs. Your recipe calls for 6 teaspoons (30 ml) of olive oil. But your teaspoon is nowhere to be found! No worries. You can convert teaspoons to tablespoons. How many tablespoons of olive oil do you need?

POUR THE PUNCH!

Sam is planning a Halloween party. He picks out pumpkins. He hangs decorations. Finally, he stocks up on candy corn. What else is left? No party is complete without a big bowl of punch!

Sam finds the perfect punch recipe. It calls for 32 fluid ounces of apple juice and 12 fluid ounces of cranberry juice. Sam also needs 1½ cups of orange juice and 8½ cups of ginger ale. But what he could use most is a new measuring jug.

The recipe lists ingredient amounts in fluid ounces and cups. These are customary units of measurement. We use the customary system in the United States. Yet Sam's jug shows only milliliters and liters. These are metric units of measurement. In the metric system, 1,000 ml = 1 liter (L). This system is used around the world.

Sam's jug used to be labeled with both units. Over time, the customary labels have worn away. So how can Sam measure his liquids?

Easy! He can convert customary units to metric units.

Sam knows that 1 fluid ounce = about 30 ml and 1 cup = 237 ml.

What metric measurements does Sam's recipe call for?

DO THE MATH!

It's time to serve the drinks! Your pitcher contains 64 fluid ounces of punch. You empty the pitcher into 10 glasses. Of course you'll make sure the glasses are filled equally. How many milliliters of punch will you pour in each glass?

WHICH LOAF TAKES LONGER?

Tisa is getting ready for her school's bake sale. She's making banana bread. She gathers her ingredients. She puts on her apron. Most important, she asks her dad to operate the oven.

First, Tisa prepares 4 cups (946 ml) of batter. Next, she looks for a loaf pan. Her parents own two. Pan A is 8 inches (20 centimeters) long and 4 inches (10 cm) wide. Pan B is 9 inches (23 cm) long and 5 inches (13 cm) wide. Tisa ponders which pan would work better.

Tisa plans to fill either pan with the same amount of batter. Yet each one has a different length and width. Her dad says this will affect the batter's surface area.

Surface area is a measurement of the surface of the batter. After Tisa pours the batter, it will stretch across the length and width of the pan. The top of the batter is its surface. Greater surface area usually means less baking time.

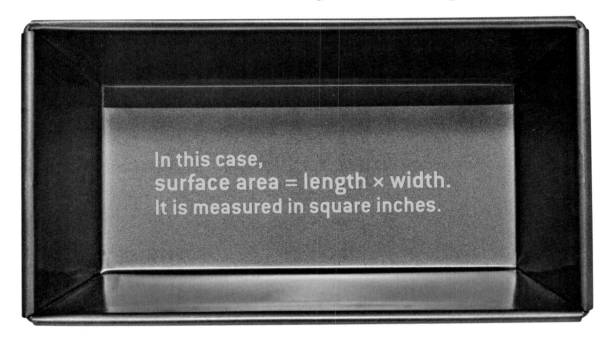

In this case,
surface area = length × width.
It is measured in square inches.

Tisa wasn't planning to do math homework. But the clock is ticking! She doesn't want to be late for the bake sale. So she needs to figure out the fastest way to finish her bread. **What is the surface area of each loaf pan? Which pan will reduce Tisa's baking time?**

BAKING DISH DILEMMA

Pilar loves starting the day with baked oatmeal squares. These breakfast bars are yummy and nutritious. This morning, Pilar is starving! She's also running late.

Luckily, Pilar and her mom baked over the weekend. They made two dishes of oatmeal squares. Pilar's mom plans to give one to the neighbors. She and Pilar can reheat the other for breakfast.

Pilar peeks inside the fridge. The dishes are slightly different sizes. Dish A is 8 inches (20 cm) long, 8 inches wide, and 1.5 inches (3.8 cm) deep. Dish B has the same length and width. But it measures 2 inches (5 cm) deep. Each dish is about three-fourths full.

Will one dish warm faster? Pilar's mom says yes! She says food with greater volume needs more oven time. Volume is the amount of space an object takes up. Volume is measured in cubic inches.

The volume of a rectangular baking dish = length × width × depth.

What is the volume of each batch of oatmeal squares? Which will warm faster?

DO THE MATH!

Smell that cinnamon? You're spooning oatmeal square batter into two dishes. You fill each to half its total depth. The batter in Dish A measures 101 cubic inches (1,655 cu. cm). Dish B measures 9 inches (23 cm) long, 9 inches wide, and 2 inches (5 cm) deep. What is the volume of the batter inside? Which batch of oatmeal squares will be done first?

Cala is visiting her Aunt Jane in England. Tonight they are making a fancy turkey dinner. Aunt Jane starts by heating the oven to 177°C.

Wait a minute! Something doesn't seem quite right to Cala. Back home, her parents always talk about temperatures in degrees Fahrenheit.

Aunt Jane explains that Celsius (C) and Fahrenheit (F) are different temperature scales. Water freezes at 32°F, or 0°C. It boils at 212°F, or 100°C.

Aunt Jane says sometimes people need to switch between temperature scales. In the United States, cooking temperatures are often listed in degrees Fahrenheit. But in England, they are usually noted in degrees Celsius.

Either way, Cala thinks their turkey dinner is delicious. She writes down Aunt Jane's cooking instructions. Cala plans to share them with her parents.

Of course, she needs to convert the baking temperature.

Aunt Jane says the formula for changing Celsius to Fahrenheit is °C × 1.8 + 32.

And Cala knows the order of operations from math class. So in this case, she will multiply before she adds. **How many degrees Fahrenheit is 177°C?**

DO THE MATH!

Turkey simply isn't the same without dressing! Let's say you have a scrumptious dressing recipe. You decide to share it with your uncle in Canada. You know that people there often measure temperatures in degrees Celsius. So you offer to find out that temperature for him. The formula for converting Fahrenheit to Celsius is (°F − 32) ÷ 1.8. The stuffing needs to bake at 350°F. How many degrees Celsius is this?

COOKIE COUNTDOWN

What's that grumbling sound? It's just Tam's stomach! She's always starving after school.

Today Tam is in for a tasty treat. She's helping her mom make oatmeal cookies! But Tam needs to be patient. The cookies have to bake for 10 minutes. Then they must cool for five minutes.

Ticktock, ticktock. Tam can't wait much longer! She spoons dough onto the cookie sheet as fast as she can. Tam's mom starts preheating the oven at 3:15 p.m. Seven minutes pass before the temperature reaches 375°F (191°C).

Finally, Tam's mom puts the cookies in the oven. Tam tries not to drool as they bake. Another 10 minutes drag by. *Ding!* A timer sounds. Her mom takes the cookies out and places them on the counter for five minutes. Their aroma fills the air.

Will Tam be able to stand the mouthwatering suspense?

What time will it be when she can finally eat a cookie? How many minutes will have passed between then and 3:15 p.m.?

IS THE ROAST READY?

Sunday is Tony's favorite day of the week. That's when he eats lunch at Aunt Megan's house. She always serves something special. And Tony always tells her she is the world's best chef.

This Sunday, Aunt Megan is making roast beef. She asks Tony to read the label on the meat. The label lists cooking instructions. It also shows the beef's weight.

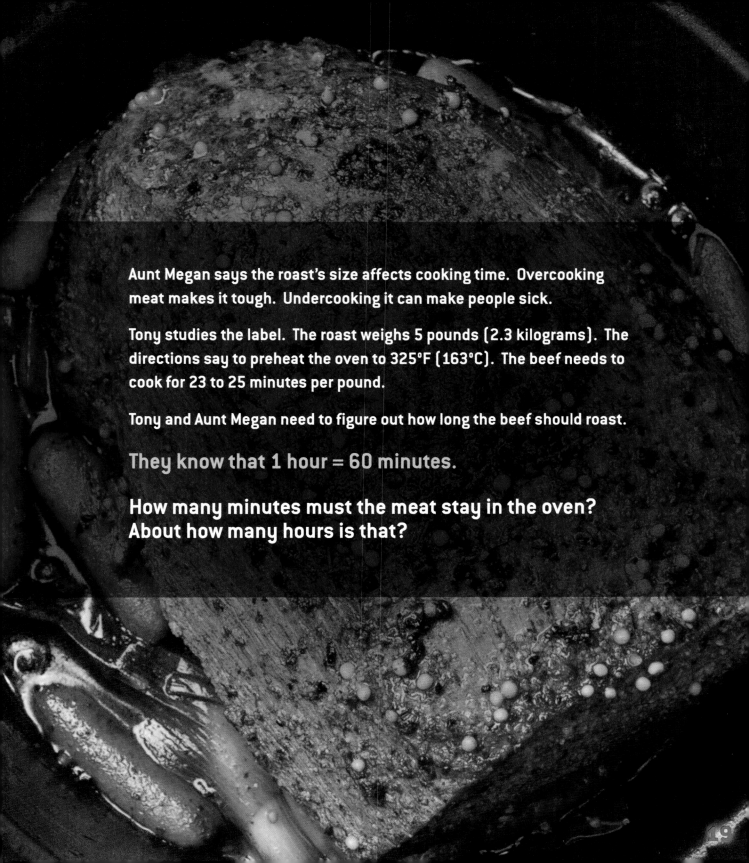

Aunt Megan says the roast's size affects cooking time. Overcooking meat makes it tough. Undercooking it can make people sick.

Tony studies the label. The roast weighs 5 pounds (2.3 kilograms). The directions say to preheat the oven to 325°F (163°C). The beef needs to cook for 23 to 25 minutes per pound.

Tony and Aunt Megan need to figure out how long the beef should roast.

They know that 1 hour = 60 minutes.

How many minutes must the meat stay in the oven?
About how many hours is that?

A TRIPLE SERVING OF SMOOTHIE

Forget boring old milk shakes! The average shake is no match for Jess and Andy's berry smoothies. Sadly, only Jess and Andy know this. They have never shared their smoothies with anyone else. All that is about to change. Today Jess and Andy are whipping up smoothies for four lucky friends.

First, they will visit the store. Normally, Jess and Andy need enough ingredients to prepare just two smoothies. Today they will increase their amounts to serve six people.

Jess and Andy review their recipe. Then they take stock. They have extra bananas, honey, and orange juice. But they are out of vanilla yogurt and blueberries.

Their original recipe calls for ½ cup (118 ml) of vanilla yogurt and 1¾ cups (272 grams) of blueberries.

How much yogurt will they need today?
How many cups of blueberries?

KITCHEN OR CANDY FACTORY?

Ray looks around his kitchen. He can't believe his eyes! Did he just wander into a candy store?

Ray's family is making fudge. His parents want to hand it out as holiday treats. They plan to share the sweetness with 18 friends. Each friend will get 1.5 pounds (680 g) of fudge.

Ray's dad mixes and heats the first batch. He pours it into a square pan. The fudge must chill in the refrigerator for three hours.

Ray wonders how long this family fudge project will take. Will they even finish before the holidays? Fortunately, his parents own four square pans. Each holds 1.5 pounds (680 g) of fudge. Ray's dad says all four pans fit inside the fridge at once.

How many pounds can Ray's family chill at any given moment? How many total pounds of fudge will they give away? How many hours of fridge time will this project involve?

DO THE MATH!

Picture your family making holiday fudge. You are preparing nine 1-pound (454 g) batches. Your job is to shop for ingredients. Your mom says she spends about $10 on 4.5 pounds (2 kg) of fudge. How much will nine batches cost?

SHRINKING SOUP

It's a cold winter day. The wind is howling. The snow is falling. What could be better than a bowl of hot vegetable soup? How about 12 bowls?

That's what Anna's grandpa might say. Anna adores his soup. So he offers to help her cook it. Yet his recipe makes 12 servings. Anna only plans to feed herself and her brother . . . and Grandpa, of course!

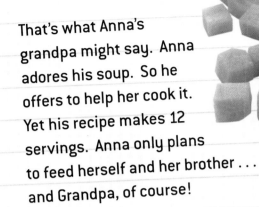

Grandpa's soup is loaded with veggies. His ingredients include four sliced carrots, two diced potatoes, and four diced celery stalks. Anna knows she must reduce these amounts. Otherwise, she'll be swimming in soup!

How many carrots, potatoes, and celery stalks should Anna slice and dice?

DO THE MATH!

Tonight you want to make vegetable soup. Your dad's recipe serves six people. Yet today, it is just you and him! So cut those servings down to two. Your dad says that he usually spends about 15 minutes chopping vegetables. How long will it take this time?

LOSE SOME LEMONADE!

Fresh lemonade! Eli is setting up a lemonade stand. His secret to success is his mom's refreshing lemonade recipe. Her lemonade is never too sour. It's never too sweet either!

Eli's mom usually makes 80 fluid ounces (2.4 L) of lemonade. She uses 8 cups (1.9 L) of water. She adds 1½ cups (355 ml) of lemon juice. Finally, her recipe calls for 1¾ cups (350 g) of white sugar.

Ack! Eli cannot find his mom's usual pitcher. She tells him it's cracked. Eli will have to serve lemonade in something else instead.

Mom's new pitcher holds only 32 fluid ounces (946 ml).

Eli knows that 32 ÷ 80 = 0.4. Or 32 = 40 percent of 80.

So he needs just 40 percent of Mom's original ingredient amounts. He will also produce only 40 percent of the lemonade she makes.

Yet changing ingredient amounts can lead to some tricky numbers! The same is true for adjusting serving sizes. Luckily, Eli has a plan. Kitchen measuring tools often feature quarter marks. He'll round to the nearest quarter as needed.

How much water, lemon juice, and sugar should Eli mix together? How many 4-fluid-ounce (118 ml) servings of lemonade can he sell?

READY, SET, BAKE!

Has kitchen math made you hungry? Well, try to silence your grumbling tummy. You have a few final questions to tackle! Don't worry. It won't take long. Solve the following problems. Then go make something yummy!

This Saturday, your school is hosting a race. Runners are raising money for a new computer lab. You offer to bring a snack. That way, everyone can enjoy a tasty reward after crossing the finish line. Your parents suggest baking bran muffins. What a perfect treat! Bran muffins are both hearty and healthful.

Your recipe makes 12 muffins. But 90 people will be racing. Clearly, you'll have to increase your ingredient amounts to make one muffin per person. Remember that changing amounts sometimes involves strange numbers. So round as needed! Your original recipe calls for the following:

- 1 cup (130 g) whole wheat flour
- 1 cup (150 g) oat bran
- $\frac{1}{3}$ cup (75 g) light brown sugar
- $1\frac{1}{2}$ teaspoons (7 g) baking powder
- $\frac{1}{2}$ teaspoon (2.3 g) baking soda
- $\frac{1}{4}$ teaspoon (2 g) salt
- $\frac{1}{4}$ teaspoon (0.7 g) ground cinnamon
- 1 teaspoon (2 g) orange zest
- 1 large egg
- $\frac{1}{4}$ cup (59 ml) honey
- 1 teaspoon (4.9 ml) vanilla extract
- 2 tablespoons (30 ml) canola oil
- $1\frac{1}{4}$ cups (296 ml) milk
- $\frac{1}{2}$ cup (83 g) raisins

How many batches should you plan to bake? How much of each ingredient will you need?

One batch of 12 muffins must cook for 20 minutes at 400°F (204°C). The muffins have to cool for five minutes before you remove them from the pan. You predict it will be roughly 10 more minutes before the next batch goes into the oven. **How long will it take to make your muffins?** Round to the nearest half hour.

Answer Key

Page 5   Maria needs 2 cups (473 ml) of chocolate syrup. (16 oz. ÷ 8 oz. = 2 c.)

Page 7   Carlo needs 12 teaspoons (59 ml) of tomato paste. (48 tsp. × ¼ c. = 12 tsp.)
He needs 4½ teaspoons (22 ml) of olive oil. (3 tsp. × 1½ tbsp. = 4½ tsp.)

Do the Math!
You need 2 tablespoons (30 ml) of olive oil. (6 tsp. ÷ 3 tsp. = 2 tbsp.)

Page 9   Sam needs 960 ml of apple juice. (32 oz. × 30 ml = 960 ml)
He needs 360 ml of cranberry juice. (12 oz. × 30 ml = 360 ml)
He needs 360 ml of orange juice. (1½ c. × 237 ml = 356 ml)
He needs 2 L of ginger ale. (8½ c. × 237 ml = 2,015 ml; 2,015 ml ÷ 1,000 ml = about 2 L)

Do the Math!
You pour about 192 ml into each glass. (64 oz. × 30 ml = 1,920 ml; 1,920 ml ÷ 10 glasses = 192 ml)

Page 11   Pan A measures 32 square inches (206 sq. cm). (8 in. × 4 in. = 32 sq. in.)
Pan B measures 45 square inches (290 sq. cm). (9 in. × 5 in. = 45 sq. in.)
The bread will bake faster in Pan B.

Page 13   The volume of oatmeal squares in Dish A is 72 cubic inches (1,180 cu. cm).
(1.5 in. × ¾ = 1.125 in., 8 in. × 8 in. × 1.125 in. = 72 cu. in.)
The volume of the batch of oatmeal squares in Dish B is 96 cubic inches (1,573 cu. cm).
(2 in. × ¾ = 1.5 in., 8 in. × 8 in. × 1.5 in. = 96 cu. in.)
The oatmeal squares in Dish A will warm faster.

Do the Math!
The volume of the batter in Dish B is 81 cubic inches (1,327 cu. cm.).
(2 in. × ½ = 1 in., 9 in. × 9 in. × 1 in. = 81 sq. in.)
The oatmeal squares in Dish B will be done first.

Page 15   The baking temperature is 350°F. (177°C × 1.8 + 32 = 350°F)

Do the Math!
The dressing bakes at 177°C. [(350°F – 32) ÷ 1.8 = 177°C]

Page 17   Tam can eat a cookie at 3:37 p.m. (3:15 p.m. + 0:07 + 0:10 + 0:05 = 3:37 p.m.)
A total of 22 minutes will pass between the time her mom preheats the oven and the cookies are done cooling.
(3:37 p.m. – 3:15 p.m. = 0:22, or 22 min.)

Page 19   The beef should roast between 115 and 125 minutes. (23 min. × 5 lbs. = 115 min., 25 min. × 5 lbs. = 125 min.)
This is about two hours. (115 min. ÷ 60 min. = 1.9 hrs., 125 min. ÷ 60 min. = 2.1 hrs.)

Page 21   Jess and Andy should use 1½ cups (355 ml) of yogurt. (½ c. × 3 = 1½ c.)
They should use 5¼ cups (816 g) of blueberries. (1¾ c. × 3 = 5¼ c.)

Page 23 Ray's family can cool 6 pounds (2.7 kg) of fudge at any given moment. (4 pans × 1.5 lbs. = 6 lbs.)
They will give away 27 pounds (12 kg) of fudge. (1.5 lbs. × 18 friends = 27 lbs.)
The project will involve 15 hours of fridge time. (27 lbs. ÷ 6 lbs. = 4.5 batches. Since the last half batch still requires the full amount of fridge time, 5 batches × 3 hrs. = 15 hrs.)

Do the Math!
It will cost about $20 to make nine batches of fudge. (9 lbs. ÷ 4.5 lbs. = 2, 2 × $10 = $20)

Page 25 Anna must slice one carrot. (12 servings ÷ 3 servings = 4, 4 carrots ÷ 4 = 1 carrot)
She needs half a potato. (12 servings ÷ 3 servings = 4, 2 potatoes ÷ 4 = ½ potato)
She must dice one celery stalk. (12 servings ÷ 3 servings = 4, 4 celery stalks ÷ 4 = 1 celery stalk)

Do the Math!
Chopping should take five minutes today. (6 servings ÷ 2 servings = 3, 15 min. ÷ 3 = 5 min.)

Page 27 Eli should use 3¼ cups (769 ml) of water. (8 c. × 0.4 = 3⅕ c., or about 3¼ c.)
He should use ½ cup (118 ml) of lemon juice. (1½ c. × 0.4 = ⅗ c., or about ½ c.)
He should use ¾ cup (150 g) of sugar. (1¾ c. × 0.4 = ⁷⁄₁₀ c., or about ¾ c.)
He can sell eight 4-fluid-ounce (118 ml) servings. (32 oz. ÷ 4 oz. = 8 servings)

Page 28 **Ready, Set, Bake!**
To make 90 muffins, you should plan to bake eight batches.
(90 muffins ÷ 12 muffins = 7.5 batches, or about 8 batches)

You'll multiply all your ingredients by 7.5. Your increased ingredients will be as follows:
- 7½ cups (980 g) whole wheat flour (1 c. × 7.5 = 7½ c.)
- 7½ cups (1.1 kg) oat bran (1 c. × 7.5 = 7½ c.)
- 2½ cups (560 g) light brown sugar (⅓ c. × 7.5 = 2½ c.)
- 11¼ teaspoons (52 g) baking powder (1½ tsp. × 7.5 = 11¼ tsp.)
- 3¾ teaspoons (17 g) baking soda (½ tsp. × 7.5 = 3¾ tsp.)
- 2 teaspoons (35 g) salt (¼ tsp. × 7.5 = 1⁹⁄₁₀ tsp., or about 2 tsp.)
- 2 teaspoons (9 g) ground cinnamon (¼ tsp. × 7.5 = 1⁹⁄₁₀ tsp., or about 2 tsp.)
- 7½ teaspoons (15 g) orange zest (1 tsp. × 7.5 = 7½ tsp.)
- 8 large eggs (1 egg × 7.5 = 7.5 eggs, or about 8 eggs)
- 2 cups (470 ml) honey (¼ c. × 7.5 = 1⁹⁄₁₀ c., or about 2 c.)
- 7½ teaspoons (37 ml) vanilla extract (1 tsp. × 7.5 = 7½ tsp.)
- 15 tablespoons (230 ml) canola oil (2 tbsp. × 7.5 = 15 tbsp.)
- 9½ cups (2.3 L) milk (1¼ c. × 7.5 = 9⅖ c., or about 9½ c.)
- 3¾ cups (530 g) raisins (½ c. × 7.5 = 3¾ c.)

It will take about 4.5 hours total. (20 min. baking time + 5 min. cooling time = 25 min. per batch, 8 batches × 25 min. = 200 min. baking and cooling time, 10 min. × 7 periods between batches = 70 min., 200 min. + 70 min. = 277 min., 277 min. ÷ 60 min. = 4.6 hrs., or about 4.5 hrs.)

Glossary

batter: a thin baking mixture made with eggs, flour, and water or milk

conversion: changing one unit of measurement to another

customary: a measurement system used in the United States. It uses the fluid ounce, teaspoon, tablespoon, cup, inch, and pound.

diced: cut into small cubes

formula: a math statement or rule that uses numbers and symbols

ingredient: a food item used to make a recipe

metric: a measurement system that uses the liter, meter, and gram

preheat: to heat an oven to a certain temperature before cooking food

surface area: a measurement of an object's total surface, or outermost layer

volume: a measurement of how much space something takes up

Further Information

Cornell, Kari. *Marvelous Muffins, Breads, and Pancakes.* Minneapolis: Millbrook Press, 2014. Put your math skills into action with the amazing recipes in this book!

IXL Math: Third Grade
http://www.ixl.com/math/grade-3
This site includes examples and practice problems to help you perfect your growing math skills.

Math Is Fun: Measurement Index
http://www.mathsisfun.com/measure/index.html
Visit this site to find answers to your measurement questions. These facts will come in handy as you cook!

Wingard-Nelson, Rebecca. *Fun Food Word Problems Starring Fractions.* Berkeley Heights, NJ: Enslow Publications, 2009.
Practice your kitchen math skills by solving these word problems.

Index